The Parks of Neenah

An Historical Interpretation

by
William E. Dunwiddie

First Edition

Library of Congress Catalog Number: 93-072914

ISBN: 0-942495-30-6

Designed by Alice D. Freeman

Printed in United States of America
by
Palmer Publications, Inc.
Amherst, WI 54406

Distributed by
Neenah Park and Recreation Commission
211 Walnut
Neenah, WI 54956

Table of Contents

Illustrations

Acknowledgements

No book is an individual enterprise. This book, like many others, has benefited greatly from the cooperation, assistance, wisdom, and generosity of many people. Several people I should like to mention gave special help and encouragement to this book, for which I am deeply grateful. Eileen McCoy, Neenah's Director of Parks and Recreation, helped locate records and minutes of Neenah City Council meetings as well as records of the Neenah Park Board and the Neenah Park and Recreation Commission. My daughter, Alice Freeman, provided both editorial support and technical assistance in preparing the manuscript for publication. Marian Wauda and Bill Zimmer of the Neenah Historical Association helped find many historical photographs and plat maps so essential to produce this work. Mary Jane, my wife, provided immediate and persistent enthusiasm for the project. Her reader reactions, faith, patience, and support nurtured me throughout the writing of this book.

In addition I am indebted to Tom Sutter, biographer of the Kimberly family, who kindly made available much information by and about Helen Kimberly Stuart. Reference librarians at the Neenah Public Library were most helpful in locating appropriate newspaper articles on microfilm. Ken Thiene of the East Central Wisconsin Regional Planning Commission kindly granted permission to use the map showing the location of Neenah parks. Fred A. Schmidt graciously permitted the use of his picture of the Neenah Lighthouse at Kimberly Point Park.

Photographs used in this book were obtained from a variety of sources. Historic photographs were largely from the collections of the Neenah Historical Association. I am grateful to the following for assistance in obtaining photographs of individuals who have helped create many of our Neenah parks. Frank Shattuck provided a photograph of his father, S. F. Shattuck; Catharine Remley made available a photograph of her grandmother, Clara Shattuck; Helen Proctor helped me locate a rare picture of her grandfather, John Proctor; the Bergstrom family kindly provided a photograph of Sara Bergstrom.

Introduction

Neenah citizens are rightly proud of the fine system of public parks that grace our community. But like other good things we enjoy—clean air, pure water, safe streets—we tend to take our parks for granted. Few realize how much planning, hard work, courage, and cooperative effort by public spirited citizens (past and present) was required to create these beautiful parks. Many are unaware that some of our finest parks and recreation facilities are the result of generous gifts of land and money from private citizens who wanted to make Neenah an even more beautiful place to work and live.

There have been two major purposes in writing about *The Parks of Neenah*. First, I wanted to help citizens of our community—particularly public officials and new members of the Neenah Park and Recreation Commission—better to understand how we got the parks we have. I have tried to write a clear, interesting, and accurate account of what private citizens and public officials have done in the past to create the fine system of city parks we now enjoy.

Second, I have tried to explain some of the policies that have been developed over time for the wise management of our city parks. The search for the story behind our parks has been a pleasant series of surprises, from park commission minutes, newspaper files, and conversations with people who knew some of the citizens who worked to create and improve our parks.

In the course of digging for fugitive facts about Neenah parks, I have discovered some interesting stories about how we acquired them. I have also learned why hard-won public parks are often threatened by sincere and well-meaning citizens and public officials who believe open space in a park might be better used for other purposes than pleasure and recreation.

The struggle to protect and preserve open space and parkland for recreational purposes is a never ending battle. Folks find it hard to understand we all have much to gain from open space and parklands. Open space helps us live healthier and happier lives—it is that simple. Of course, it is hard to place a dollar value on our personal health and happiness, but no one can deny they are valuable and important goals for each and everyone of us.

A careful reading of our park history makes it clear why we should value citizens who work to protect and preserve open space and parklands. They really help each of us protect and preserve our own health and happiness! Can any civic effort be more worthy?

From *The Parks of Neenah* much can be learned to guide us in the wise development and management of parklands. If we know little of the history of our parks, we are likely to repeat past mistakes. Knowing something of the difficult struggle to create and preserve open space and parks may help us to appreciate them even more than we do now.

The Village Green—Our Oldest Park

Most people value grassy meadows and open space; no one likes to feel confined or crowded. If there is not enough useful open space, we work to create it. We clear forests, drain marshes, develop parks and playgrounds. In 1843 Neenah's pioneer settlers decided to protect and preserve a grassy meadow in the village. In doing so, they gave us our first and oldest park.

Many of those who came to settle in eastern Wisconsin hoped to farm. They were disappointed to find so much land unsuitable for farming, covered with trees and bushes. There were few naturally open, treeless places to build homes, pasture cows or plant crops. One of their most immediate and pressing needs was to find pasture and hay for livestock. Often the best natural grasslands were river meadows, and fortunately there were grassy meadows along the Fox River. The open meadows along the river probably attracted some of the early settlers to our community.

Many of our pioneer settlers were Yankees from New England states where there were also few natural grasslands. There it was the custom to set aside a piece of land in (or near the center of) the village called 'the commons', or 'the Green'. It was a public or common pasture open to all, where any herdsman could pasture cattle and livestock. In 1843 some early settlers in the Village of Neenah set aside one and six-tenths acres of land as a commons or village 'green'. Our 'Green' (now known as Columbian Park) is fourteen years older than famous Central Park in New York city.

First known as Public Square Park, the meadow was probably used as a common pasture or hayfield. The park provided open space for kite-flying and simple games, but the area wasn't even fenced until 1884. Records show the Neenah Park Board was paid for hay harvested from the Public Square in the 1890s. From 1900 to 1929 it was the Neenah High School football field. Today it contains a softball diamond, and the center of the park is flooded in winter for skating. The ice rink is lighted and supervised. The heated shelter provides a warm room for skate-changing. There are teeter-totters, swings, slides, and a sandbox. In 1921 two tennis courts were built for $250 at the urging of C.B. Clark.

So, from humble beginnings, a common pasture and hayfield has been turned into a neighborhood park. 1993 marked the 150th birthday of 'The Green', one of the oldest parks in Wisconsin!

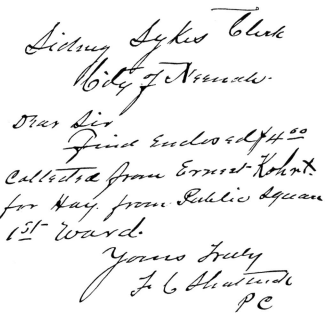

Figure 1. Public Square Park was little more than a hayfield in 1889.

Laudan Fields—Our Second Oldest Park

Pioneers never found new land conveniently labeled as farmland, homestead, grist mill site, church, cemetery, pasture, or playground. Each landowner had to envision the various ways to use a given piece of land, and always there were more possible ways to use land than the owner could even imagine. The poor landowner, with limited means and experience, had no clear plans to guide him. He might try and fail at several ways to use his land before he stumbled on a use that was good for him and his community.

To determine the best use for privately owned land was never easy, but it was even more difficult for a community to agree on the best ways to use public land. This land was often left over after private owners had acquired what was regarded as the best property available. It was often less desirable land to build on; maybe it was too wet or rocky, too heavily wooded, poorly located, or the soil lacked fertility. It was the land least wanted, or perhaps it was land set aside for a street. It could not easily be used to make money. Such was the case with Laudan Fields.

Laudan Fields were on the south edge of the Village of Neenah in 1856 when the community gained possession of this property. The land shows up on an 1857 map as an area between what was then known as North Park Street and South Park Street.

The land may have been a gift to the village, but the legal record is somewhat obscure. The fields, renamed *Bigelow Park*, were farmed and used to grow hay into the 1890s. On the 1909 Neenah map shown in Figure 2, the area between the two Park streets is clearly labeled as PARK for two blocks west of Oak Street and two blocks east of Oak Street. An eastwest boulevard between Higgins Avenue and Elm Street was never built as a boulevard, although the name, Laudan Boulevard, remains on the street.

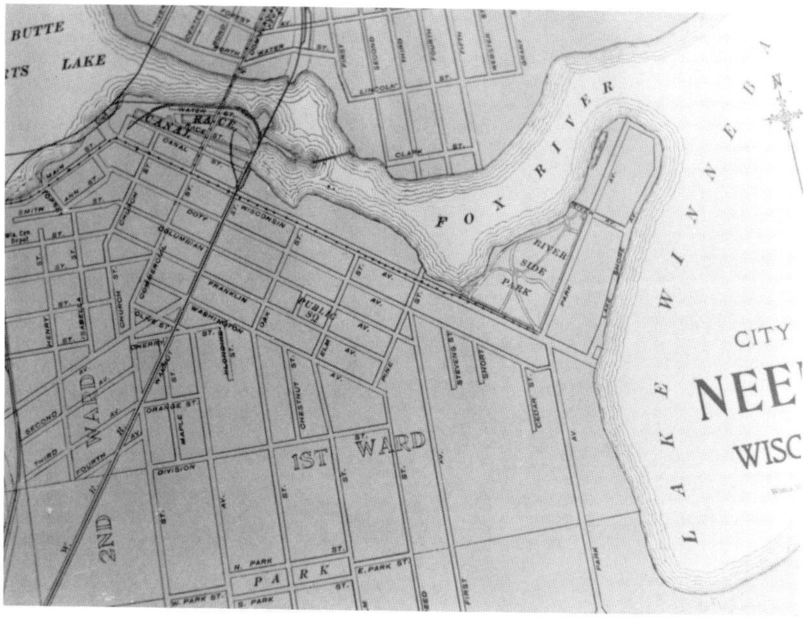

In April 1932, the Neenah Park Board was instructed to drain Laudan Fields, and then to level, grade, and seed the area. This was part of the City's make-work program for the winter of 1931-1932. It was estimated the cost of this program was about $1500.

As Neenah began to grow southward following World War II, the city fathers decided in 1947 to sell part of Laudan Fields to the School District for the construction of Wilson Elementary School. Bigelow

Figure 2.   City map showing the PARK.

Park was reduced to about one acre, considerably smaller than a good neighborhood park should be.

Fortunately, Arthur Bohnen offered to sell to the city three lots he owned west of Oak Street, about 600 feet along Laudan Boulevard, and adjoining the new school property. How he got title to land that had belonged to the City since 1856 is not clear, but Bohnen did sell the land back to the city for about $4000. This accounts for the present two acre size of Laudan Park.

The shelter in Laudan Park was designed and built in 1965 by the Superintendent of Parks, Tom Baer, and his crew.

A Christmas Gift to Ourselves—Riverside Park

Lumberman Henry Sherry loved the Fox River; that much was clear. He had built his very successful new sawmill and lumber yard on the south banks of the river on Wisconsin Avenue. He owned more than 100 acres of choice waterfront property along the Fox River and Lake Winnebago at the point where the Fox River leaves the Lake. These sizable land-holdings gave him an idea.

Early in 1872 he made an offer to the Neenah Village Board to sell fifteen to twenty acres of land on Warner's Point, immediately adjacent to Wisconsin Avenue, for a public park. Further, he proposed "to lay out and construct a drive, turnpiked and graveled, along the shore of Lake Winnebago from near the ice house [present site of Rec Park] to the Old Council Tree [west of the present Light House], following down the bank of the river and intersecting the park grounds, a distance of a mile and a quarter around."

Henry Sherry's offer provoked much debate, and the Village Board handled the offer like a political hot potato—with great caution. Some citizens thought the price of $4400 ($220 per acre) was way too high, especially for something as frivolous as a park.

Far-sighted citizens like John Proctor (half-owner of Neenah's biggest flour mill) braved the criticism of many of his contemporaries.

He strongly supported buying waterfront land for a public park.

It was said of him later that "more than to any other citizen of his time, belongs the credit for saving for all time this choice property for the benefit and enjoyment of

John Proctor

untold generations." His granddaughter, Helen Proctor, reported that her grandfather particularly liked the idea of the drive along the lakeshore. In fact, he urged the Village Board to buy the entire point of land north of Wisconsin Avenue (for about $6000), but his argument fell on deaf ears.

Figure 4. Riverside Park about 1872; note the Council Tree.

The Editor of THE NEENAH GAZETTE, Charles Boynton, strongly urged his readers to support the purchase of Riverside Park. On June 22, 1872 he wrote "there surely is not a more delightful place in Winnebago County for a park than this spot. Nature seems to have lavished of her rich abundance a bountiful supply of lovely attractions. One of the finest groves of second growth hickory, elm, and maple cover the entire grounds; while the placid waters of the mouth of the channel of the Fox River, skirting along the entire north and west side, with a high dry bank, lends a charm that cannot easily be excelled."

Boynton ridiculed those who thought Neenah already had enough parks. He wrote "it is objected by a few that we have parks, already appropriated, one in Bigelow town, [the Green] and one in Jones plat [west end of the island]. Is it possible, that we have a single intelligent reader, that

seriously calls these two parcels of land, parks! Not a vestige of shade, not a shrub, or tree marks their existence. They serve their present purpose as cow pastures, and cannot be used to better advantage without an immense outlay of time and money. At Riverside, we have everything in readiness to occupy at once, and the most pleasant spot in all the country." [THE NEENAH GAZETTE, June 22, 1872]

The Neenah Village Board, amid considerable discord and charges of extravagance, was not easily persuaded to purchase the twenty acres for Riverside Park. It was so unsure of what to do that it decided to make a small down payment ($300) of 'earnest money' to hold the land, and made the full purchase contingent upon its approval by the voters in a referendum.

Despite the cold of Tuesday, December 24, 1872, the decision whether or not to purchase the land for Riverside Park was put to all the male voters of the village. A fairly good turnout voted 141 *For*

Figure 5. Dock and pavilion in Riverside Park, circa 1890.

the Park purchase, 84 *Against*. So Riverside Park became in fact, a Christmas gift to ourselves!

In the early days Riverside Park became a mecca for steamboat excursions from other cities. In 1895 the Corps of Engineers dug a deeper channel (illustrated in Figure 6) immediately off-shore from the park to make it easier for the big steamboats to land passengers. At the same time the Corps removed a part of The Point that extended northwest from its present location to improve navigation in the Fox River channel as shown in the map in Figure 7. A wood dance hall was built in the north part of the park (donated by Henry Sherry—June 12, 1885). There was also a shelter for picnic tables and outdoor toilets.

For the first eighteen years safe drinking water was apparently unavailable in the park. The Park Board wrote in their 1890 Annual Report, "we wish to say that in our opinion the well we sunk last December and tiled up in good order will furnish our people with pure water at all times, which is something that has been needed since the opening of the park."

Figure 6.   Boats in the Fox River channel.

Over the years many children have enjoyed climbing on the cannon in Riverside Park. They may have imagined the park was well defended. Actually the 4.7 inch Howitzer received from the War Department in 1920 was "not considered safe for firing." That gun

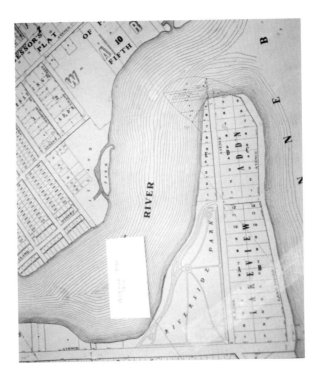

Figure 7.   Riverside Park and The Point.

was contributed to a scrap drive in World War II, so the park was without a cannon for a few years. In 1948 the War Department offered to provide a 37mm Japanese anti-aircraft gun for the park, but local sharpshooters shot down the offer as being "too small and it would look out of place." So the Chief of Ordnance offered to switch guns, a bigger military trophy, a 75mm gun made in Japan! Local gunners, eager to get "a bigger bang for the buck," were delighted, even though shipping costs for the 4000 pound monster had to be paid by the City.

In 1932 Phelps Wyman of Milwaukee, an eminent landscape architect, was hired by the Park Board to redesign Riverside Park. His plan illustrated in Figure 8 called for the original drive, that more closely followed the shoreline, to be moved to its present location. Wyman also visualized a new

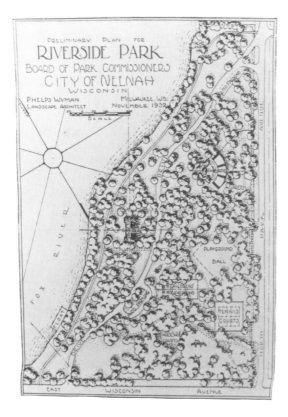

Figure 8. Riverside Park map by Wyman.

park pavilion facing west in the deep bend of the drive, embodying all needed features, such as restrooms, kitchen, stage, dance floor, and space needed by yachting enthusiasts, particularly during regattas. This multipurpose summer pavilion became a reality in the summer of 1956 through the generosity of a neighbor to the park, Mrs. Vina Shattuck Beals. Since 1957 the pavilion has provided a 260 seat theater in-the-round for Neenah's summer theater company, *Riverside Players*.

Riverside Park was enlarged during the years 1968-1984 when 420 feet of valuable riverfront land on the north side of Wisconsin Avenue west to Pine Street was added to the park. This was made possible by the gen-

erosity of Mrs. Beals through a trust under her will.

Riverside Park is by far Neenah's most heavily used park. A 1992 survey of citizens indicated eighty-one percent of respondents used the park. Communityfest celebration takes place at Riverside Park each 4th of July. The park's 19.9 acres have 2050 feet of shoreline along the Fox River, from which citizens can view the famous Venetian Parade and the fireworks.

In July 1993, the sculpture-fountain *Playing in the Rain* by Neenah native, Dallas Anderson was unveiled in Riverside Park. Privately funded, *Playing in the Rain* represents ten children in various stages of play during a summer shower. Surrounded by a shallow pool, the 'rain' falls around the sculpture at pre-determined intervals.

The models for the sculpture were chosen from hundreds of local children interviewed by sculptor, Dallas Anderson—each selected to represent different ages and stages, portraying 'the wonder of childhood'. The figures are just over life-size, positioned at varying heights among and on five bronze columns.

Playing in the Rain, in the words of its sculptor, is "dedicated to the children of the Fox Valley and children throughout the world . . . a work of art that [is] a celebration of childhood, an eloquent reminder that memories are forever preserved on the retina of the heart."

Neenah Mayor, Marigen Carpenter, in accepting the gift on behalf of the city said, *Playing in the Rain* is "an artistic expression of the cherishing of our children." In short, she said, "It is art that warms the heart."

See Figure 48 on page 47 for an aerial view of Riverside Park.

Wasteland Becomes Shattuck Park

Like many of us, Clara Shattuck was disgusted by man-made ugliness. Every time she walked by the rubbish that littered the property north of Wisconsin Avenue just east of the railroad tracks, she was newly offended. Unlike those who chose to ignore the eyesore, she made up her mind to create a place of beauty where only ugliness prevailed. Shattuck Park was her beautiful and lasting gift to our community.

Over the years the site that became Shattuck Park had been abused. It had been used by a sewer pipe company, a marble works, a coal yard, a boat works, and a steam laundry. Part of it was a swamp, and by 1910 it had become nothing more than a rubbish dump. (See Figure 10 and Figure 11.)

In February 1912, Clara Shattuck bought

Clara Shattuck

the site to develop a public park. Not only did she purchase this valuable riverfront wasteland, but she generously provided funds to clean up the site and build the park. She had the park designed and built with a lagoon near

Figure 10.   View of Wisconsin Avenue swamp.

the eastern end where the swamp had been, and a concrete retaining wall along the entire 400 feet of waterfront and surrounding the lagoon. A beautiful pavilion was built in the northwest corner of the site. It included boat stalls, and a building designed and equipped as a boat factory and livery. A boat dock, walkways, and driveways were built, and the park was completely landscaped with trees, ornamental shrubbery, lawn, and flower beds.

The completed park was deeded to the city of Neenah by Clara Shattuck on August 26, 1915. The city ordinance (No. 332, Vol. 3) accepting Shattuck Park stipulated certain conditions governing the management and use of the park. The first condition said "the city of Neenah . . . shall forever care for and keep in proper repair all structures and permanent improvements . . . including lawn, trees, ornamental shrubbery, seats, buildings, retaining walls, dock, lagoon, window flower-boxes, and harbor, in such a manner as to maintain and augment the beauty and usefulness thereof as a park and dock open at all times to the public."

One provision in the Shattuck Park ordinance became public policy for *all* Neenah parks. As a condition for accepting the park, Clara Shattuck required the city agree that "no intoxicating liquors of any kind shall be sold, given away, drunk, used or stored [in the park] at any time."

Figure 11.   Remains of the old steam laundry.

Although occasionally some citizens have questioned the ban on alcoholic beverages in our parks, long experience shows countless unpleasant problems have been avoided by following this prudent policy.

Neenah has indeed been fortunate to have had citizens with foresight like Clara Shattuck. She seized the opportunity to create beauty from what had been an unsightly refuse dump. She made her dream of a beautiful public park come true, and in doing so, gave a permanent gift of beauty to our community. Neenah is a better place to live and work and play because of her.

Fresh Air Camp

We can be fairly certain School Nurse Sarah Conner never dreamed of a lakeshore park with a fine sandy beach when she first suggested an open air school to the Board of Education. Yet it was from her original recommendation that the idea of our Fresh Air Park began to grow.

There are parks that develop as part of a deliberate plan, and others that seem to just happen. Some parklands are gifts to the community, others are purchased with public funds. Some property is clearly identified for park purposes from the beginning, while other property seems more suitable for other uses. Fresh Air Park just happened to become a public park; it was never a part of any long-range plan. Incredibly today it is part of our Neenah Park System.

Fresh Air Park did not start out as a park and is not even within the corporate limits of the City. It began as a Fresh Air Camp on the shores of Lake Winnebago, run by the Neenah School District, on land purchased by the City. It was fully twenty-seven years later (1947) that the City Council turned over the property to the Neenah Park and Recreation Commission to be operated as a park.

The conventional wisdom in 1919 was that fresh air and sunshine were good for your health, especially if you suffered from tuberculosis. So when Sarah Conner, School Nurse for the Neenah Schools, recommended the School Board establish an 'open air school', the proposal received friendly consideration. The School Board hired Phyllis Taylor (salary—$1050) to be the first full time teacher, and budgeted $800 to purchase necessary equipment.

Strange as it may seem, the first class of twenty children in the Fresh Air School met in the Auditorium Room of the City Hall. The stuffy air of the old City Hall evidently did them no harm, for the School Nurse reported in April 1920, that the children in the Fresh Air School gained an average of about five pounds in the first thirty days.

As might be expected, the Fresh Air School soon moved out of doors to a Fresh Air Camp located on Lake Winnebago about a mile south of Neenah near Rainbow Beach. In June 1921, the City paid $600 for two, sixty foot lakeshore lots with a wonderful sand beach. It was an excellent site for a summer camp for children. From gifts of lumber and materials, volunteers built a new building on the property to provide a kitchen and dining rooms for the greater number of children at the camp that summer. (THE DAILY NEWS, June 27, 1921)

The Fresh Air Camp was operated until 1936, and the frame buildings were removed about 1941. The property was turned over to the Neenah Park and Recreation Commission in May 1947. In 1972 about fifty feet of waterfront property was added to the park for $5000, and one acre of land between the park and Maple Lane was purchased in 1974 for $21,000. Total area of the park is about 1.68 acres with 180 feet of shoreline.

Fresh Air Park provides one of the few points of public access on the west shore of Lake Winnebago. The sandy beach, one of the few on the lake, has long been popular with swimmers, especially during the dog days of summer. It is unguarded, a swim-at-your-own-risk beach, but it is very shallow for several hundred feet from shore, making it fairly safe for families with little children.

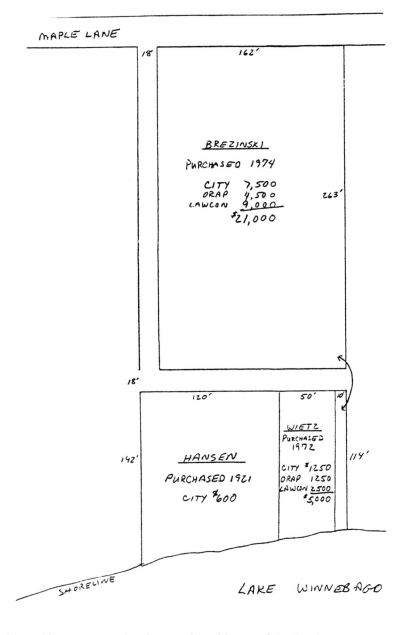

Figure 12.   Map showing purchase history of Fresh Air Park.

A boat ramp provides access to the lake for fishermen with small craft, and it is an important route onto the lake for ice fishermen in the winter. For the safety of swimmers, the boat ramp is closed during June, July, and August.

Over the years Fresh Air Park has produced more than its share of problems, mainly late night beer parties. It is difficult for Neenah police to provide adequate surveillance due to its location, more than a mile beyond our city limits. Several attempts have been made to turn the park over to Winne-

bago County for a county park, but county officials have been unwilling to assume responsibility for the park.

In Fresh Air Park, Neenah has a small but valuable parcel of waterfront property on the shores of Lake Winnebago. The fine sandy swimming beach is a unique feature that greatly adds to the recreational value of this property. By giving badly needed public access to Lake Winnebago, Fresh Air Park has a value far beyond what its size would suggest. It is good example of how "small can be beautiful!"

A Park for Doty Island

C.B. Clark believed public parks and playgrounds should be readily available throughout the community for all to enjoy. He had the idea they should be located so that young and old alike would have easy access to a neighborhood park. His actions revealed his convictions. He helped give not just one but *two* fine waterfront parks to our community. Doty Island Park on the banks of the Fox River was the first; Recreation Park on the shores of Lake Winnebago was the second.

Figure 14.　　One of the bridges in Doty Park.

C.B. Clark

Charles Benjamin Clark, Jr. was founder of Theda Clark Memorial Hospital. One of our most public spirited citizens, he was, like his father, a former Mayor of Neenah. Prior to 1922 much of the property we know as Doty Park was a low marshy wetland, frequent-

ed by turtles, frogs, muskrats, ducks, and little boys hunting all the above. Clark's father had purchased it many years earlier with the idea that one day he or his family might build a home on the site.

In 1922, Clark (and the other heirs to his father's estate) gave approximately five acres of the land to the city with the stipulation that it be used entirely for "park and playground" purposes. A group of individuals added to Clark's gift with the purchase of several frontage lots on Lincoln Street. This greatly improved public access to the park. First known as Island Park, it is 9.25 acres and includes about 1200 feet of Fox River shoreline.

Because most of the property was cattail marsh, considerable fill was hauled in to

Figure 15. Doty Cabin—the Grand Loggery.

bring low spots up to a grade-level dry enough for park purposes. Some fill was obtained from a lagoon that was dredged through the lowest part of the marsh. This created an island that added a charming feature to the park. Two graceful bridges were built that are attractive to artists, photogra-phers, and young bicyclists. Five tennis courts and a shelter building were added later. Records show that by 1931 more than $56,000 had been invested in Doty Island Park construction. In 1985 a new stone shelter building for Doty Park was a gift to the city from Mrs. Dorothy Pickard.

In 1925 Mrs. John Strange offered "to give to the City of Neenah the Governor Doty Cabin now located on my homestead . . . ." The city accepted her offer, the cabin (shown in Figure 15) was moved to the park, and the park was renamed Doty Park. The Grand Loggery, the name Mrs. Doty gave to the home of Wisconsin's second Territorial Governor, James Duane Doty, houses a growing collection of historic artifacts, some dating back to an even earlier period.

The Secretary of the Park Board, S.F. Shattuck, noted that "the opening of Doty Island Park corrected an imbalance of public parks in the city. There had been a growing desire on the part of island residents for a park on Doty Island. The construction of Doty Island Park was in line with the policy of the Park Board to build a park for each major section of the city."

See Figure 49 on page 48 for an aerial view of Doty Island Park.

Thank You, Mrs. Stuart!

The story of Kimberly Point Park is inevitably linked with Helen Kimberly Stuart. Every public park needs friends like her. She was one of the most forward-looking, public spirited women of her time. Kimberly Point Park, one of our most beautiful waterfront parks, was her lasting gift to our community. There simply would be no park at the Point today were it not for her determined fight to create the park and protect access to it.

Helen Stuart was a formidable community leader with a long list of accomplishments. Although Wisconsin women had won the right to vote in 1920, few were eager to take part in the "dirty game of politics."

Unlike most of her fellow citizens, she was not content to be merely a spectator of political affairs. She welcomed the opportunity to run for public office. Helen Stuart was the first woman elected to the Neenah Board of Education. Elected in 1930 by an overwhelming margin, she was the first woman to serve on Neenah's City Council, Plans Commission, and Library Board. She ran unsuccessfully for Mayor of Neenah, the first

Helen Kimberly Stuart

woman to try for that office. She was clearly a political trailblazer.

The Neenah League of Women Voters was started by Helen Stuart, and in 1929 she served as President of the State League of Women Voters. She was appointed a member of the Board of Regents of the University of Wisconsin, and was selected to serve as a State Regent of the Daughters of the American Revolution. In 1948 she founded the Neenah Historical Society, and her longstanding concern for the welfare of Native Americans was well known.

Helen Kimberly Stuart enjoyed a good political fight. She liked few things better than to wage a successful political battle for a good cause. Few were more proud of Neenah than she; none worked harder to preserve

Lake Shore Drive and to beautify and improve Park Point.

In March 1928, Helen Stuart was disturbed to learn from her alderman that her next door neighbor, F.J. Sensenbrenner, president of the Kimberly-Clark Company, was planning to build a million dollar estate on what was known as Park Point. Her alderman told her that Sensenbrenner was quietly obtaining options on every property on Lake Shore Drive and North Park Avenue with the plan to buy all the land east of Riverside Park and north of Wisconsin Avenue to the Point.

Like most of her fellow citizens, she assumed land acquired in 1925 by the City would always be public parkland. This property, then known as Park Point, was two lots

F.J. Sensenbrenner

wide, 120 feet deep north and south. The two lots extended the whole width of Park Point east and west. The land occupied the northern most part of the Point, bordering both the lake and the river.

She saw clearly that Park Point could not serve as a public park if there was no way to get to it. Keeping Lake Shore Drive open was absolutely necessary to protect Park Point for the people.

Helen Stuart eagerly led the fight to protect Lake Shore Drive and preserve Park Point. Although her next door neighbor was the wealthy and influential president of the biggest paper company in town, she was not afraid to oppose him. It is likely he found her both determined and intimidating. Knowing how much Lake Shore Drive and Park Point meant to the community, and driven by an apparent personal dislike for Sensenbrenner, she decided to try to block his plan to build a home on Park Point.

Her first move in the fight over Park Point was a Letter to the Editor of THE

NEENAH DAILY NEWS-TIMES

OPEN FORUM

March 17, 1928   page 3

Editor News-Times—

Cititizens of Neenah, wake up. Save the Lake Shore Drive for the city!

How many of you know of the plan on foot to close off the Lake Shore Drive north of Charles Hintertheur, east and west from the lake to the river? What a calamity to Neenah! What would become of the crowds who watch the Regattas on race week? What would become of one of Neenah's greatest assets? What is it visitors to Neenah are always shown first? What is it we are proud of?

The plan if carried out would start a precedent that would in time shut off all the shore line from the end of Wisconsin Avenue north, for if you allow the mayor and council to close the Lake Drive for one person, you will have no reason for not closing it for all.

GET BUSY TODAY! See or call up your mayor and your councilmen and stop this loss of the highway that attracts the tourists, the Regatta crowds, and is a delight to every one of your own citizens. Make the Lake shore a beauty spot for future generations.

See to it that the city does not dispose of its right of way.

Wake up, Citizens of Neenah! Save your Lake Shore Drive for your City! The taxes you would get from a residence on that property would be nothing compared to the loss of money in years to come to our merchants, restaurants and hotels by the loss of tourists when we have sold our birthright for a mess of pottage!

Here is a cause for public spirited citizens to take up.

Signed—A Tax Payer.

REPORT PARK POINT LAND IS OPTIONED

Question of Lake Road Involved in Rumored Negotiations

According to reports current in real estate circles here for several months but persistently denied by all parties concerned, all of the lots east of Riverside park on the point adjacent to the mouth of the Neenah branch of the Fox river in the north east half of blocks D and C have been optioned for F. J. Sensenbrenner, president of the Kimberly-Clark company.

Rumor also persists that if the options obtained are taken up, Mr. Sensenbrenner plans the erection of a palatial residence. Several acres of ground are included in the tract.

Mr. Sensenbrenner denies that the options on the land, which have been secured by the George J. Mayer company of Menasha, are for him and also that he intends building a residence there.

Public interest in the reported transaction has been aroused because of the question of the city's highway right-of-way bordering the lake which might become involved.

The lots both east of North Park avenue and west on the bank of the river are included in the land reported to be optioned. About two years ago the city acquired from Charles Briggs portions of several lots on the northwest end of the point which make acessible to the public a portion of the lake shore.

Figure 18.   NEENAH DAILY NEWS-TIMES articles.

13

DAILY NEWS-TIMES on March 17, 1928, illustrated in Figure 18. She alerted her fellow citizens to the threat to close off Lake Shore Drive, and shut off all access to the Lake Winnebago shore line from the end of Wisconsin Avenue north. She urged citizens of Neenah to get busy, see or call your mayor and councilmen. "Save your Lake Shore Drive for your city" and future generations.

Nowhere in her letter did Helen Stuart identify by name who was trying to close Lake Shore Drive to the public. But it was easy to learn his identity because in the same issue of THE DAILY NEWS-TIMES, page one, he identified himself! As shown in Figure 18, Sensenbrenner denied that the options on the land were for him. He also said he did not intend to build a residence on the Point.

Next Helen Stuart organized a delegation of women to appear at the meeting of the City Council on March 19, 1928 to protest the possible closing of Lake Shore Drive. According to Mrs. Stuart, Mayor Dennhardt had worked quietly to persuade all but one lakeshore property owner to agree to close off Lake Shore Drive. He would ask, "Wouldn't you rather have a beautiful million dollar estate on the Point than the way it is?" However, at the Council meeting that night, he changed his tune. The Mayor was reported to have said "the idea that some people have that this road or any other would be closed is ridiculous. Too much of the Lake shore is closed to the public now."

Someone, possibly Helen Stuart, took the unusual step of inviting City Attorney Mitchell of Oshkosh to address the Neenah City Council. He said he could not conceive of any Council giving away or selling the road. He explained that a unanimous vote of the aldermen is needed to vacate any street, lane, or alley, and the ground for such action is on proven necessity or on benefit to accrue to the city.

Much controversy arose over the effort to block F.J. Sensenbrenner from building a palatial residence on the Point. Citizens who feared the city would lose much needed property tax revenue from a million dollar home were highly critical of Mrs. Stuart. They didn't know (nor did she reveal) what she suspected, that he intended to give the home to his church (as a home for old priests) with permission for him to live there as long as he wished. Church property, of course, cannot be taxed. If the home belonged to a church, he could live there tax free, and the city would be unable to obtain any tax revenue from this choice property. Sensenbrenner later did build his new home across the lake on property next to the North Shore Golf Club. He did, in fact, give his home to the church, as Mrs. Stuart anticipated.

In August 1928, Edward Sherry (the only son of Henry Sherry who sold the land for Riverside Park to the City) gave to the City by quit claim deed all the land the family had retained between Lake Shore Drive and the Lake from Wisconsin Avenue to Park Point. The deed contained an important proviso. "This deed . . . is given under the specific condition that the City of Neenah shall not at any time sell or dispose of any land or interest in land which it secured by virtue of this deed, but shall devote it to public park purposes."

Park Point was still small, 120 feet deep and two lots wide. Mrs. Stuart had hoped to create a bigger park at the Point. One year later, in April 1929, she presented to the City four remaining lots to be added to Park Point under the following conditions:

"The land . . . is to be used permanently, continuously and forever for public park purposes, and public park purposes only, and to be maintained and properly kept up as part of the city park system . . .

"That 'Lake Shore Drive'. . . be permanently, continuously and forever maintained as a public street throughout its entire length, in its present location . . .

"That said park shall continuously, constantly and forever be named and called 'Kimberly Point' or 'Kimberly Point Park'. . . in commemoration of [her father] John A. Kimberly . . . ."

Helen Stuart continued to maintain her lasting concern for the park by providing $200 per year for five years for expenses of upkeep of the park. In 1932 she paid for twenty elm trees to be planted in Kimberly Point Park, and later provided money for the flowering crabapple trees that are so beautiful every spring. In 1948 Mrs. Stuart gave an additional gift of $3000 to widen the driveway, increase the parking area, construct four stone fireplaces, provide eight picnic tables, and certain pieces of playground equipment.

The Kimberly Point Lighthouse has become a famous landmark on Lake Winnebago. It was a gift from James C. Kimberly. Made of brick and Haydite block, it rises more than forty feet above the river channel. It began to guide boaters into the Neenah harbor in September 1945.

In April 1991 a handicapped-accessible fishing dock was completed at the Point at a cost of $34,000. Eighty per cent of the cost of this park improvement was provided by the Scenic and Urban Waterways Program from the Wisconsin Department of Natural Resources.

Public parks are inevitably linked with controversy. Even when a park is a gift "for the enjoyment of all the people," a few citizens will object because park development and maintenance costs will be an unwanted burden. Or some will cry over the lost property tax revenues when the land becomes publicly owned.

That is why parks need friends, and the more the better. Parks need friends who value open space and parklands, not for the privileged few, but for everyone. Parks need friends to defend and protect them from

Figure 19. The Lighthouse by Fred A. Schmidt.

private citizens and public officials who would like to see parkland put to other uses.

Those who manage public parklands should remember, parks need informed friends. In the struggles to create and improve recreational facilities and parklands, the more informed citizens (like Mrs. Stuart) who will join the fight for better parks and playgrounds, the better the chances for success.

An aerial view of Kimberly Point Park is included in Figure 50 on page 49.

A Gift to the Children of Neenah—Washington Park

Mrs. Sara Bergstrom wanted to give the children of her community a lasting gift of a playground or park. She was an elderly widow in her seventies when she decided to make this dream a reality. She got in touch with S.F. Shattuck, Secretary of the Neenah Park Board, and explained what she hoped to do. One point

Sara Bergstrom

was made clear at the outset, she wanted no publicity or recognition for this gift. Her identity was to be kept secret.

S.F. Shattuck was the perfect choice to negotiate for the Park Board. At the time,

probably no one was better informed about park and recreational needs of the community. He too, preferred to do good deeds quietly and without any publicity, so he readily agreed to keep her identity secret.

He knew the Park Board had long been aware a playground was needed in the Fourth Ward. In fact, earlier a tract of land along Winneconne Avenue had been sought by the park board. But while the need for acquiring public land was recognized, as was the need for a playground, either finances had been lacking or satisfactory terms could not be made with owners.

Shattuck explained to Mrs. Bergstrom that if she would agree to support the plan to develop a park in the Fourth Ward, the city would obtain options on three parcels of land desired for the playground. Knowing we tend to value a park more dearly if we have helped to pay for it, Shattuck probably suggested that the city itself put at least $5000 into the project. To further prevent public knowledge of her identity, he suggested the donor of the money for the playground insist that deeds for the three lots to be purchased be given directly from the present owners to the city.

Sara Bergstrom must have appreciated the help and guidance provided by Shattuck for she followed his suggestions exactly. The minutes of the City Council for Wednesday, October 7, 1931 report that "His Honor, Mayor George Sande, stated that for some time the Park Board has been working on the securing of land for park and playground purposes in the Fourth Ward; that the Park Board had been offered the sum of $15,000 by an individual of the city to purchase a suitable site, provided the city would furnish an additional $5000 to cover part of the cost and improvement of the same. The Park Board had agreed on a site [off Winneconne

Avenue, west of Harrison] and options had been secured pending action of the Council."

A unanimous vote of the Council appropriated $5000 for the purchase and improvement of land for park and playground purposes in the Fourth Ward, and the Mayor and City Clerk were instructed to write a letter of appreciation for the gift.

The headline in THE DAILY NEWS-TIMES on October 8, 1931 read **"Aged Woman Gives $15,000 to City for City Playground."**

The report spelled out details of the terms of the gift. "The terms of the gift are so made that development of the tract immediately is assured. They provide that $10,000 of the $15,000 is to be used toward purchase of the land, the $5000 appropriated by the council completing the purchase price. The other $5000 of the gift is set aside for the beautification and development of the tract as a playground and park."

The terms of the gift may seem insignificant at first, but they reveal the guiding hand of an experienced park developer. Shattuck knew if there were no funds for development and beautification of the tract, it would lie idle and useless. He knew how hard it would be to get development funds, especially in 1932, the worst year of the depression. Mrs. Bergstrom's generous gift (roughly equal in today's dollars to about $100,000) would not by itself have been sufficient to provide for development and construction of the park. Everyone, including the donor, would have been disappointed. So the terms of the agreement were carefully designed to reserve funds for development of the park.

Ordinarily building a park this size would extend over several years, and the cost would be spread over several capital improvement budgets. But the city's need for work projects during the depression helped to compress into a short time what would otherwise have been a long process.

S.F. Shattuck

For one month in 1932 the Fourth Ward Park bore the name of H. J. Lewis Park. Lewis was the last remaining veteran of the Civil War, Grand Army of the Republic. But Shattuck thought to check with Sara Bergstrom on a name for the park. He told the Park Board on July 13, 1932 "that the donor of the property for the Fourth Ward Park suggests the name 'Washington Park' for this area . . . ." After some discussion the Park Board rescinded its earlier action, and officially named the new park Washington Park.

Washington Park was designed primarily for play. Its eastern edge along Harrison Street was laid out with playground equipment. Four tennis courts were fitted into the southwest corner along Winneconne Avenue. A lighted softball field holds center stage, and the swale is used for an ice rink in winter. A modest size sledding hill has been built in the northwest corner of the park, where a heated shelter building is located to serve both skaters and sledders. Our community is forever indebted to Sara Bergstrom for helping make this fine park a living reality.

An aerial photo of Washington Park may be found in Figure 51 on page 50.

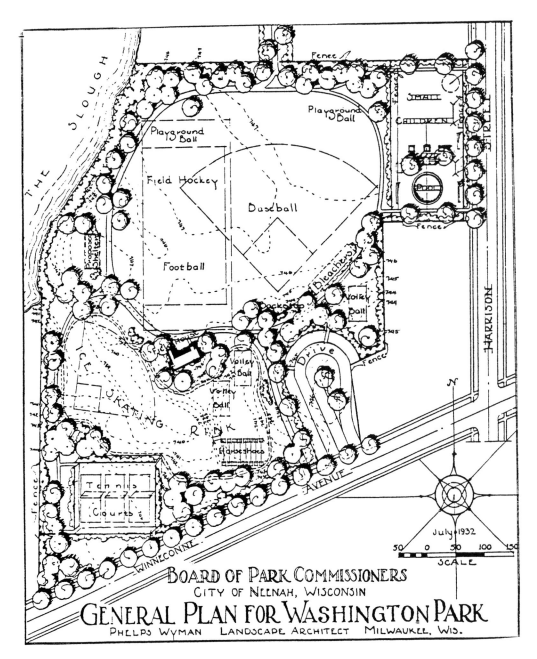

Figure 22.   1932 Map of Washington Park.

Hard Times Helped Create Island Park

The property we now identify as Island Park began life as a cattail marsh. At first it was never intended to be a park or playground. When the city began to fill in the marsh in 1931, there were no laws to protect and preserve wetlands. It was strictly a make-work project to create jobs for the jobless.

Sometime prior to 1925 a concrete retaining wall was built across a small marsh on the north bank of the Fox River. It extended from the west end of Lincoln Street about 650 feet to the east end of the Chicago and Northwestern railway bridge. The wall was probably intended to protect the bridge from erosion by spring floodwaters. North of the retaining wall a cattail marsh of about 1.8 acres was cutoff from the river.

In the worst days of the economic depression of the 1930s, unemployment in Neenah was serious. The City Council was eager to find any make-work projects that would create temporary jobs for the jobless. In so doing, the Council hoped to reduce the number of people in need of relief assistance.

The minutes of the City Council for May 6, 1931 reveal that one alderman suggested "in hiring laborers [for this project] the contractor be instructed to hire only Neenah men, and that married men be given preference." At the same meeting the City Clerk was directed to "advertise for bids on 8,000 to 15,000 cubic yards of fill to be delivered in back of the retaining wall below the Neenah dam." The estimated *difference* of 7000 cubic yards suggests the Council really had no clear idea of how much dirt would be required.

The land behind the concrete retaining wall below the Neenah dam was little used at first. But it didn't take long for fishermen to realize there was good fishing off the wall, especially in early spring when the water was high. Neighborhood children found the open space a good place to play games, fly kites, and do all the things kids do in a park. So the property was used as a play area even before any development took place.

Figure 23. Fishermen along fence at Island Park.

A chain link fence built along the top of the concrete retaining wall marked the first step in building the park. Rest rooms were added later, and the very first sledding hill in any of our Neenah parks was built in Island Park about 1965. Kids with sleds showed up with the first snow flakes that winter! Small sledding hills have proven so popular that the Park Board decided every park should have its very own sledding hill! Unfortunately, most Neenah parks are still without one.

Figure 52 on page 51 shows Island Park from the air.

A Pool with a View—Recreation Park

Locally lots of folks, young and old, like to fish or swim. Surveys show water sports easily lead the list of favorite outdoor activities. Fishing is heavily favored by men, while swimming is strongly preferred by women. Sports like hunting, golf, tennis, and bowling all trail far behind. These facts help to justify the need for a strong water safety program in our community and a public swimming pool where the required skills can be learned.

Figure 24.   The bath houses on the lakeshore.

Swimming has long been popular in Neenah. On one hot June day in 1921, THE DAILY NEWS reported "the hot weather of the past few days has had a marked effect on the daily patronage of the municipal bathing beach near the water works. Sunday when the heat wave reached its peak, was the banner day at the bath house. Best estimates place the number of bathers at well above the two thousand mark . . . ."

Lake Winnebago has its good days and its bad days, but like the little girl with the curl, when it is bad, it is horrid! The lake flies that hatch twice each summer are a harmless nuisance. But they can make it difficult to breathe without inhaling the critters. In late summer when water temperatures rise in the seventies, an excessive bloom of green algae often makes the lake smell bad, look bad, and be unfit for swimming. The Winnebago Indians, in fact, long ago gave the big lake an appropriate name—*Stinking Water*.

The City Council minutes for May 18, 1937 reveal there were further difficulties for those who wanted to swim in the lake. The public bath house on the lakeshore (shown in Figure 24) was in bad condition. The Council was told "something should be done so that it would not be necessary to spend so much money each year on repairs . . . ." The bath house was too close to the lakeshore. It was being ruined by the ice-push each spring, and it was suggested "if the building was moved back 20 feet or more, this condition would not exist." The beach was also hard to walk on barefoot; "the stones along the present

C.B. Clark   S.F. Shattuck

beach should be removed, and filled in with sand; this would make a great improvement to the bathing beach."

Fortunately for our community, two citizens were ready, willing, and able to improve conditions for local swimmers. In February 1938, C.B. Clark and S.F. Shattuck, offered anonymously to help the city build an Olympic size outdoor pool on the site of the old public swimming beach.

Figure 26. Neenah Pool Construction—1940.

It was estimated that the construction of the outdoor pool and recreation building would cost about $140,000. The two donors offered to give the choice lake shore site to the city, and they further agreed to pay $52,000 of the cost if the city would provide $25,000. The balance of $63,000 was provided by a grant from the Public Works Administration.

Mayor Ed Kalfahs was delighted to announce the plan for a new pool to the Council, and he strongly urged the Council to accept the offer. He pointed out the present public beach was not adequate, especially since the Water Works buildings had been enlarged. He reminded the Council that the city had for some years considered securing other waterfront property for municipal bathing purposes. He said "the city's cost [for the new swimming pool] was very nominal, in fact, it would be only about [equal to] the cost of the land . . . The cost of the pool project would be paid out of surplus, and it would not affect the tax rate."

The Mayor must have been dismayed at the initial response of the Council. Alderman Schmidt said "he thought the pool and buildings were too elaborate, and that the revenue from users of the pool would not equal the expense of operation." Alderman O'Brien urged caution in accepting the gift, and said the plan for a pool should be put to a referendum of the voters. Alderman Heigl said he thought the pool, which he understood would accommodate about 200 swimmers at one time, "was not large enough for a city the size of Neenah." The resolution before the City Council was to accept the offer to convey certain lakeshore real estate to the city of Neenah for a municipal swimming pool. It also accepted the offer by the owners of the real estate to pay two-thirds of the cost of the swimming pool; authorized payment by the city of one-third of the cost of the project, not exceeding $25,000; and directed the city to proceed with the project. On May 4, 1938, the Council passed the resolution by a vote of eight to two.

Figure 27. Neenah's Olympic-size pool.

Finally, in the summer of 1940, more than 70,000 swimmers, mostly Neenah children and adults, took their first swim in the new municipal pool. One of the most pleasant features of the new pool was the superb views of Lake Winnebago from the balcony above the west side of the pool. It was truly a pool with a view!

In the winter, a toboggan slide, as shown in Figure 28, was built on the roof of the boys locker room, making the site useful more of the year.

Thousands of children have learned to swim and acquired water safety skills at the pool since the summer of 1940. That in itself is enough to justify the city building and operating this municipal pool. But we must never forget that the pool and Recreation Park were made possible by generous gifts of land and money from C.B. Clark and S.F. Shattuck.

Figure 28.   Toboggan slide at the pool.

Certainly the city would never have acquired these fine recreational facilities without their help.

Figure 53 on page 52 shows aerial views of Rec Park and Quarry park.

How a Weed Patch Became Cook Park

Near the end of a long, hot summer, Mrs. Jessie Buck was probably tired of fighting weeds on her property. She wrote a letter to the City Clerk "offering to sell [her] land adjacent to River Street and West North Water Street [to the City of Neenah] for $1000 and Perpetual Care of a cemetery lot."

The Common Council Minutes for Wednesday, August 7, 1940 report that "after discussion Alderman Loehning moved that the offer of Mrs. Buck be rejected and that she be notified to abate the public nuisance [weeds] existing on such property" or the city would cut the weeds and charge the cost to her. "On a call of ayes and noes motion prevailed all voting aye."

The west end of the island, commonly known as 'Dogtown', had lots of children but no public park or playground. Knowing a play area when they saw it, children on the island often played on the empty weed-covered lots. In September 1940, two of the aldermen talked with Mrs. Jessie Buck and Mrs. William Oehlke about buying their land for playground purposes. They reported to the Council "they had a price of $850 on Mrs. Buck's property, and $325 on the Oehlke property." On September 18, 1940, the Council voted unanimously to purchase the properties for $1175. It is interesting to note that island children were among the first to see the possibility of making Mrs. Buck's 1.8 acre weed patch into a public playground!

Samuel A. Cook

For more than fifty years Cook Park has served the west end of the island as a small neighborhood park. The Park and Recreation Commission has long wanted to increase its size by acquiring properties immediately adjacent to the park, but it was not until 1992 that the park was enlarged by three-tenths of an acre. One small house and lot were purchased for $33,000, one-half funded by Land and Water Conservation (LAWCON) funds. The house was in excellent condition, and with low cost housing scarce in Neenah, it was made available to Habitat for Humanity for relocation in the city.

Cook Park illustrates two basic rules for park development:

1) *A neighborhood park should be at least five acres in size and within a fifteen minute walk (or one-half mile) of citizens of the neighborhood.* Cook Park is only about one-half the size it should be, but it is within a fifteen minute walk of many citizens (especially children) at the west end of the Island.

2) *Every public park or playground should have easy public access from every side.* No one should have to cross private property to gain access to a public park. All of our island parks (Doty, Island, and Cook) and Douglas Park (near South Commercial) have private property immediately adjacent to the park that tend to block easy public access. The city should be ready and willing to acquire any such property that might become available.

Cook Park was named for an outstanding citizen of Neenah, Samuel A. Cook. He was an 'Islander' who lived from 1881 until his death in a beautiful home on the banks of the Fox River on the present site of the Neenah-Menasha YMCA. In 1888 Cook was elected mayor of Neenah, serving the city with great success for one term. In 1889 he was elected to the Wisconsin State Assembly where he served until 1894 when he was chosen to represent the Sixth Congressional District in the United States Congress.

Figure 30.   Playground equipment in Cook Park.

Cook was remarkably successful in business, particularly in the Neenah Paper Company which he acquired in 1887 in partnership with Henry Sherry. He was one of the first in the country to adopt a successful plan for profit-sharing with his workers. In 1906 he presented the community with a generous gift of the S.A. Cook Armory, home of Neenah-Menasha Company I of the Wisconsin National Guard. Many of the early Neenah-Menasha basketball games were played in the Armory.

At his death on April 4, 1918, THE NEENAH DAILY TIMES said of him "it is not often given to a man to have the deep affection of a community as Mr. Cook had. No one will ever know how generously he gave of his time, his advice, his sympathy and his means to those who needed help . . . He found pleasure and recreation in doing things for others and he did them modestly and unobtrusively, because he loved to."

It is most appropriate that Cook Park bears the name of a man who was dearly loved by his community. It is a lasting tribute to this worthy man; every community could use more citizens like Samuel A. Cook.

Our Most Cleverly Hidden Park

Most Neenah parks are easy to find and have good public access. Douglas Park is an exception. It has been so cleverly hidden away that few local citizens know where it is or how to get to it.

The site was originally purchased by the city as a possible future location for a city garage. But the city later found it to be too small for a garage site, and access in and out for trucks and equipment was far too limited. Since no one else wanted the land for anything, the city decided in 1949 to turn it over to the Park Department for a neighborhood park.

Douglas Park is a small triangular shaped neighborhood park of 4.3 acres. The long side (hypotenuse) of the park runs from southwest to northeast, parallel to a railroad track. The railroad tracks pretty well block access to the park from west and north.

The east edge of Douglas Park runs parallel to South Commercial Street. The park is almost completely hidden from view from Commercial Street by nine private homes. The city in 1972 purchased for $992 a narrow twenty foot strip of land to give direct access off Commercial Street. Heavy traffic on Commercial Street tends discourage users from the east. The south side of this triangular park runs east and west, parallel to Douglas Street. Ten homes along that street effectively block access to the park from the south. One fifty foot en-

Figure 31.   View looking north of shelter in Douglas Park.

trance strip provides access from Douglas Street.

It is no wonder that Douglas Park is perhaps our least used neighborhood park. Few can find it, and those that do discover it is remarkably inconvenient to gain access.

A contest was held in 1961 to name what was then called Second Ward Park. Two children received awards for submitting the name *Douglas Park*.

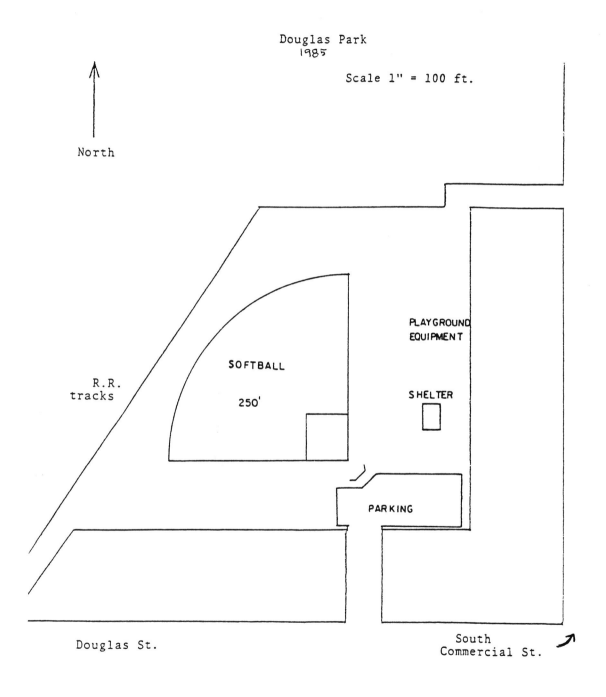

Figure 32. 1985 Map of Douglas Park.

Douglas Park demonstrates the importance and value of long-range planning in finding and reserving suitable sites for parks and playgrounds. It is far better (and much less expensive) to identify future park sites *before* private urban development has claimed all the choice land.

Wisconsin municipalities now have the legal right to designate on street extension maps the future right of way needed for streets beyond the city limits. It is equally important for a community to be able to designate and acquire possible future park sites beyond the borders of the city. It would be a much less expensive way to protect and preserve open space, and obtain land for future parks.

Neenah's Biggest Park—Memorial Park

From early on, Neenah's plans for growth and expansion had to deal with an obvious fact. The city could grow in only two directions, west and south. Lake Winnebago blocked expansion to the east, and Menasha blocked growth to the north. In 1962 a choice piece of farmland lay directly in the path of Neenah's westward expansion.

Henry Swatscheno's 160-acre farm bordered Tullar Road on Neenah's west city limits. It was a beautiful farm, roughly square, with a half mile frontage on Tullar Road. About in the middle of the west edge of the farm was a twenty acre woodlot that had never been grazed. Swatscheno was willing to sell the farm to the city at a fair price ($950 per acre), provided he could continue to live on his farm until he died.

It is rare for such a large piece of property to be available for any city to purchase, right on the edge of town. More likely a developer would have acquired the property, with plans to divide it into lots to sell for a handsome profit.

Figure 33. Playground equipment at Memorial Park.

Memorial Park was created out of Henry Swatscheno's farm. It is by far the largest park (105 acres) in our park system. It came to be a park as a result of some shrewd and effective *joint-planning* by the Park and Recreation Commission and the Board of Education.

For a number of years the Park and Recreation Commission had urged the city to purchase land for future park development on the west side of town. The City Council had completely ignored these requests. But at the time the Swatscheno farm became available, a new fact had to be considered in plans for orderly development of Neenah's west side. The Board of Education was also looking for land for a Junior High School and a site for a High School. It made good sense to combine these requests for land for parks and schools.

Jens Sorenson (for the Park Commission) and Paul Groth, (School Board President) talked over the matter and saw it was best for the parks, the schools, and the community if they joined together to present their land acquisition needs. Like the United Way, they agreed "to put all their begs in one askit!" The combined request was too big to ignore. The City Council could not help but agree that the purchase of the farm was a wise and prudent investment.

In December 1962, the city purchased the Swatscheno farm for $152,000. In 1964 it sold a fifty-five acre rectangular section of the farm along Tullar Road to the Neenah Joint School District for $66,000. Twenty acres in the northeast part of the property were used as a site for Conant Junior High School. Thirty-five acres immediately south of the Junior High School were set aside for the site of a senior high school, built in 1972. This left 105 acres to be used for park and recreational purposes.

In 1964 the Park and Recreation Commission strongly urged the city to build an indoor-outdoor swimming pool as an integral part of the new Junior High School. A new pool was badly needed to ease the overcrowding at the Neenah Pool in Recreation Park. More than $100,000 could have been saved by coordinating the building of the school and the new pool.

The Park Commission pointed out that if

the pool were built as an integral part of the new school, approximately one third of the cost of the pool would be borne by citizens in the outlying townships. The Board of Education favored the plan and gave it their endorsement. The total cost for a new indoor-outdoor pool, suitable for year-round use, was estimated in 1964 at about $400,000. Unfortunately the City Council rejected the plan as an extravagant scheme the city could ill afford.

Henry Swatscheno so loved the land he added a proviso to the deed making his farm the property of the city. He asked the city to dedicate a minimum of fifteen acres of the woodlot as a public recreation facility. It was to have a bronze dedication plaque. The

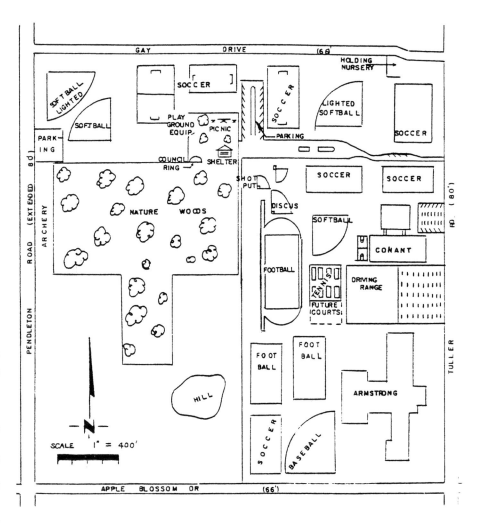

Figure 34.   1990 Map of Memorial Park.

plaque is located in the northeast corner of the woods near the park shelter. The Swatscheno Nature Woods and the Park Shelter were dedicated on May 19, 1974.

The shelter was a $62,000 gift from an anonymous donor. $48,000 in LAWCON funds paid for bringing sewer and water lines into the shelter from Tullar Road. The high cost for sewer and water was due to limestone ridges encountered between the shelter and Tullar Road.

The Memorial Park shelter includes provision for a nature center. The Swatscheno Nature Woods is about twenty acres in size. It is particularly beautiful in May when trillium, spring beauties, and dogtooth violets carpet the woods in abundance.

The Neenah Lions Club gave $5000 to develop a playground area in the park, and John Sensenbrenner, Sr. donated $5000 for

Figure 35.   Henry Swatscheno admiring the plaque.

Memorial Park development. A large sledding hill in the southeast corner of the park and a playground fort northwest of the shelter building are special features made possible with these gifts.

An aerial view of Memorial Park is shown in Figure 54 on page 53.

A Dairy Farm Becomes Southview Park

Good parkland is hard to find. Most good park sites are long gone by the time a community decides to look for a desirable site in a particular part of town. The few possible sites are often seriously flawed. They are too rough, wet, or inaccessible; or too badly abused or too expensive to develop. Too frequently they are sites no one else wanted.

Fortunately in 1965 when Neenah began to realize the need for a neighborhood park in the southwest part of the city, good land was still available.

The Wilms farm, located just south of Bell Street between Bruce and Marathon Avenue, was for sale. It was twenty-seven acres in size of which about eight acres were wooded. It was an ideal site for a neighborhood park,

almost exactly where the Park Commission would have wanted a park site to serve the recreation needs of citizens in that part of town.

It seemed almost too good to be true that a fine park site was available exactly where and when it was needed. However, just because a good site was available didn't mean the city was willing and able to buy it. Public spending for parks and recreation is widely regarded as a low priority need. Park officials must present stronger justification for park proposals than that required for other public services.

The Park Commission was aware the Board of Education was looking for a site for an elementary school somewhere in the southwest part of the city. *Joint-planning* (as in the

Figure 36. Wilms Woods with dairy cattle in 1965.

LAWCON/ORAP funding. The two little league baseball diamonds and batting cage were built and paid for by Neenah Baseball. The open picnic shelter in the woods was built by a work crew from the Wisconsin Conservation Corps.

Figure 55 on page 54 shows an aerial view of Southview Park.

case of Memorial Park) helped convince the City Council that a twenty-seven acre park could meet two needs at the same time—the need for a park and the need for land for an elementary school.

On April 6, 1965 the City Council, by unanimous vote, directed the City Attorney to negotiate the purchase of the Wilms farm. The price per acre was more than double that paid for the Swatscheno farm three years earlier. The total price paid was $58,000, $2500 per acre for the eight wooded acres, and $2000 per acre for the remaining nineteen acres.

Fine recreational facilities have been developed at Southview Park. Six lighted tennis courts have been built, partly financed with

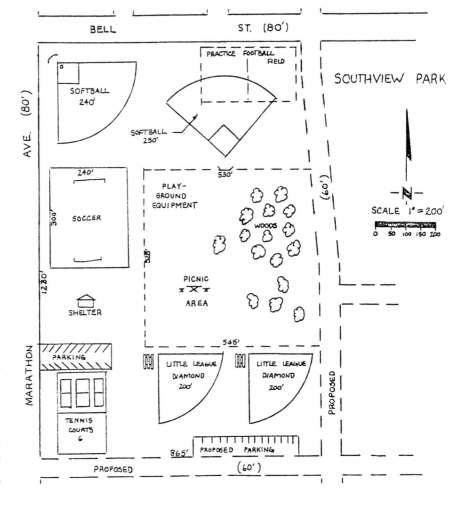

Figure 37. 1990 Map of Southview Park.

29

Can a Cattail Marsh be a Park?

Wilderness Park is a unique twenty acre natural wetland area in the southeast corner of Neenah. Many folks probably don't even consider it a city park because it doesn't look like one. There is no playground equipment, no softball or soccer fields, nothing to help identify the area as a park. What does catch your eye is the luxuriant cattail marsh!

More than two-thirds of the park (about fourteen acres) is covered by cattails, crowded in together so densely that little else can grow there. The marsh dominates the park to such an extent that it controls how the park should be developed. Since it was acquired in 1971, more marshland was added to the park area, and the excessive growth of cattails has completely crowded out the small ponds that once attracted ducks to feed and nest there.

Wilderness Park was bought by the city in 1971 for $27,500. Half the funds were provided by the Federal Land and Water Conservation fund, and twenty-five percent came from state funds. In 1990 almost five acres (mostly marsh) were added to the park by gift and quit claim deed by Winnebago County. However, if you viewed the park today (1993), you would find little evidence that any money has been spent to develop or improve the park.

For almost twenty years the development of Wilderness Park was largely neglected. There were several reasons for this. First, bigger and more heavily used parks were given a higher priority by the professional staff and the Park and Recreation Commission. Scarce public funds were used to develop and improve better known parks.

Second, with two-thirds of Wilderness Park a cattail marsh, the normal pattern for park development did not fit. Everyone agreed it should be kept as a natural wetland wildlife area, but the staff and the Commission had no experience in how to develop such an area. There was little public interest in the park, even among those who knew where it was. As a result, staff time and energy and public resources were directed toward more heavily used parks where there was greater public interest and concern.

Third, the cattail marsh posed particularly vexing problems. The 1980 development plan for Wilderness Park aimed to restore and improve the wetlands. Wildlife ponds were to be created in the cattail marsh. The wildlife ponds had to be six to seven feet deep to ensure a permanent water supply, and they were to be of sufficient size (at least 1.5 surface acres) to attract a diversity of wildlife species. The problem was how to get the cattails out of the marsh, and what to do with them once they were removed. Efforts to control the cattails and restore the wildlife ponds were notably unsuccessful.

Wisconsin wetlands once covered more than ten million acres, but for most of our history they were drained and filled with careless abandon. Today only a tiny fraction of once vast marshes and wetlands remain. Water, of course, is absolutely essential to all living things. Wetlands reduce water pollution, improve water quality, and help increase supplies of fresh water. Wetlands help control floods, and they support abundant and diverse plants and wildlife. Unfortunately the importance of wetlands is not widely understood or appreciated, mainly because so little is known about them.

Fortunately, here in our own backyard, we have a twenty acre wetland (Wilderness Park) that could be developed into an excellent nature center for the study of wetlands and wildlife observation. If we hope to preserve and protect wetlands,(or any natural areas or parklands), we must help citizens know them, for the better an area is known, the less likely it will be destroyed. The Senegalese conservationist Baba Dioum has said, "*In the end we will conserve only what we love, we will love only what we understand, we will understand only what we are taught.*"

The fact Wilderness Park is mostly wetland is precisely what makes it such a unique and valuable park for our community. If properly developed as a nature center for the study of wetlands and wildlife, it could help citizens of all ages learn to know and appreciate the need for and importance of wetlands. In teaching citizens to value and respect natural areas, this park could become one of the most important in the Neenah park system.

An aerial view of Wilderness Park is shown in Figure 56 on page 55.

Neenah's Phantom Park

Our strangest city park is an idle lakeshore landfill on the south shore of Little Lake Butte des Morts. It could be one of our most attractive waterfront parks, just west of downtown Neenah. Young and old alike who have no neighborhood play area nearby would be delighted to have a park in this spot. But for reasons none foresaw, this promised parkland—Arrowhead Park—has been nothing but an illusion for more than forty years.

It all began in December 1950 when Nathan Bergstrom made an exciting proposal to the Neenah City Council. The Bergstrom Paper Company needed a landfill area to dispose of its papermill waste. He presented an artist's sketch of a future park, showing boat docks, a spacious park pavilion, children's playgrounds, baseball fields, tennis courts, and a large parking lot.

Bergstrom proposed a park be developed on land created by filling in the south end of the lake with de-inked papermill waste. This waste was a gray wet sterile sludge made up mostly of clay and tiny cellulose fibers so small they slipped through the screens on the paper machines.

Bergstrom indicated the City of Neenah would need to obtain title to thirty-two acres of submerged lake bottom from the State of Wisconsin. He said the City would be asked to lease about four acres of the filled land to Bergstrom Paper Company for the purpose of installing equipment for the treatment of its de-inked papermill wastes. This seemed to be a reasonable request, for the company needed space for building its waste treatment plant.

The proposal solved a critical problem for the Bergstrom Paper Company—where to dump its papermill waste. It was under orders from the Department of Natural Resources to reduce pollution of the Fox River resulting from effluent from its paper machines. At the

Nathan Bergstrom

Figure 39.   Proposed park development plan—December 1950.

same time new land would be created for a park on a choice waterfront site, and the site would give a new point for public access to Little Lake Butte des Morts. Just about everyone present at that City Council meeting thought the proposal seemed to be a great idea.

Early in 1951 the City asked the Wisconsin Legislature to authorize the land transfer, and the State of Wisconsin deeded some thirty-two acres of lake bottom in the southwest corner of Little Lake Butte des Morts to the City *"for a public purpose."*

On July 2, 1951 the City of Neenah leased a 3.29 acre parcel of this landfill area to the Bergstrom Paper Company for the erection of a waste water treatment plant. It was estimated at the time it would take about fifteen years to fill the thirty-two acres. In 1970, 1974, and again in 1983 the Bergstrom Paper Company asked the City to lease additional land for its own private use, and in each case the City agreed to do so.

In October 1973, Bergstrom Paper Company offered to hire a landscape architect to develop

park plans for the landfill area, as shown in Figure 40. The City Council accepted the offer. Shattuck, Siewert, and Associates were hired, and in cooperation with the Neenah Park and Recreation Commission, park development plans were prepared. They included amusement rides, a boat launch, a sledding hill, fishing piers, baseball diamonds, playing fields, tennis courts, picnic areas, and a park shelter.

The architect reported to the Park and Recreation Commission that less land was available for a park than they had been led to believe. Somehow two acres (roughly equal to two football fields) had disappeared, and no one could explain the loss. The familiar expression "use it or lose it" seemed to apply. The plans had to be redrawn when it was discovered only about twenty-three acres remained for park purposes. Although the thirty-two acres were not completely filled and covered with a layer of topsoil, the park project (now reduced in size) moved slowly ahead.

In March 1975, after almost twenty-five years of unofficial status, the Bergstrom landfill site was officially designated as a

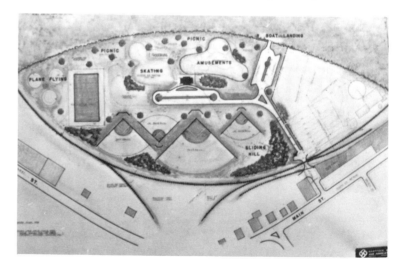

Figure 40.   1973 Bergstrom landfill park development plan.

public recreational area by the Neenah City Council. The designation meant the Neenah Park and Recreation Commission was given jurisdiction of the land when fill operations ended and a dirt cover was placed over the acres of sludge.

As the landfill neared completion, several problems arose. It was unclear who should pay the costs for closing the site. When the Department of Natural Resources (DNR) issued the order for abandonment, which meant no more sludge could be dumped in the landfill, the DNR required a two-foot layer of clay and six inches of topsoil be placed over the entire area. The dirt cover was needed because the sludge and clay papermill waste deposited in the landfill was sterile. Grass, shrubs and trees would not grow. It was estimated more than 75,000 cubic yards of topsoil would be required, and dirt was by no means cheap.

In July 1975, the City of Neenah and Bergstrom Paper Company came to terms on a cost sharing plan for closing the landfill. No more than a one-foot layer of clay was deemed sufficient by the city and the Bergstrom Paper Company, so they refused to put more clay and topsoil to cover the fill.

In 1980 an even more serious problem arose. The DNR ordered tests to analyze the sludge dumped in the landfill-park site. Few were aware the sludge buried in the landfill contained some highly toxic polychlorinated biphenyl (PCB) deposits. PCBs were found in six of nineteen samples at levels higher than fifty parts per million, the Federal standard defining a hazard. A letter from the DNR in June 1982 recommended that "the City of Neenah not proceed with further development of (Arrowhead Park) until additional information is obtained . . . ." This letter effectively put a stop to any development of the area as a park.

To make this area safe for park use, additional fill is necessary to bury the contaminated soil adequately. Until now, the DNR has been reluctant to define how much more fill will be needed.

Since 1951 the Bergstrom Paper Company (now P.H. Glatfelter) has used an ever bigger share of the new land created on the south shore of Little Lake Butte des Morts. Overall the City has leased (or lost) more than one-third of the original thirty-two acres in the landfill. The paper company has gradually reduced Arrowhead Park to only 19.56 acres, fifty-six percent of what was first promised.

Although the Wisconsin Legislature clearly stipulated the land was to be used "*for a public purpose*," the paper company was permitted to lease more than 10.5 acres of valuable lakefront property for its own private uses and at little cost. Public access to the lake, and to what was left of Arrowhead Park, was blocked by the land leased to the paper company. The City simply chose to ignore the stipulation that the land be used "*for a public purpose.*" Not until 1983 did the City belatedly begin to charge a modest rent ($12,000 per year for twelve years) for the use of this choice waterfront site.

Arrowhead Park is today a park in name only. A truncated sledding hill and a boat launch are all that reveal what was once to have been an attractive waterfront park. KEEP OUT signs warn off any who might like to explore the park.

Arrowhead Park stands as a warning for those who believe that once an area is designated a park, it will become a park. New parks and old are often threatened by public officials, leaders in industry, and ordinary citizens who believe they see better, more profitable ways to use open space.

Figure 57 shows an aerial view of the Arrowhead Park site on page 56.

Baldwin Park

Baldwin Park is a 2.9 acre park that was given to the city in 1975. It is an 800-foot strip of land on the east banks of the Neenah Slough along Baldwin Street.

It has swings, a slide, and sandbox. There are a couple of picnic tables and benches, but the trees in the park are too few, and too young to provide much shade on a hot summer day. This park is in a part of the city that has been short-changed for parkland and open space.

Figure 41.   Playground equipment in Baldwin Park.

Quarry Park

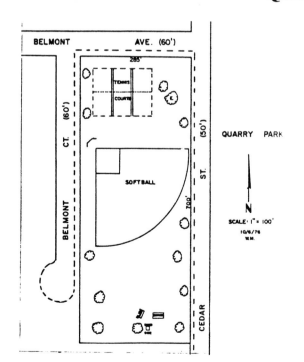

Quarry Park began life as a hole in the ground, a stone quarry for limestone. Later in the 1950s it was used as a city dump, and the quarry gradually filled with refuse. In 1973 it could no longer serve as a dump, so the city covered it with fill and rubble, and turned it over to the Park and Recreation Commission for a park.

Quarry Park includes about five acres of rather rough ground, especially the part that is over what was formerly a city dump. It is minimally equipped as a playground, and its biggest and best feature is the excellent sledding hill.

Figure 42.   Development plan for Quarry Park.

Whiting Boathouse

The Whiting Boathouse was a gift to the city in 1956 from George Whiting. He loved high speed powerboats of which he had owned several. He intended that his Boathouse would provide a home for the thirty foot long Neenah Police Boat. For many years the Police Boat was kept at the Boathouse, until the boat developed dry-rot. It has been replaced with a smaller craft, which is still kept in this building.

The Boathouse is a popular place for parties and receptions. It is the most heavily used rental facility in the parks.

Figure 43.   The Whiting Boathouse.

Tolverson Corner

In 1965 the Tolverson property immediately east of the Neenah Public Library was up for sale. It was small, only about half an acre, but it had 120 feet of shoreline on the Fox River. It might have gone to a private developer had not S.F. and Ruth Shattuck promptly bought the property and given it to the city. They recognized it was worth more to the community as a small park, than for it to be put to any other use. It is a refreshing bit of open space in a crowded part of the city.

A New Concept in Parks—Bill Miller Park and Trail

Our newest park is named in honor of the late Bill Miller, Director of Parks and Recreation in Neenah for 37 years. It is located in the Mahler Farm subdivision, on the city's southeast side. The idea for the park was proposed by Paul Hoffman, developer for the Mahler Farm subdivision.

The newest park includes a 1.5 mile fitness trail that contains a dozen different exercise stations and a grove of trees indigenous to Wisconsin. The trail occupies about 3.9 acres, and starts from a small three acre public park in the center of the subdivision. The fitness trail includes a six foot wide paved walkway to make it accessible to the handicapped, bicyclists, and roller bladers.

In the southwest corner of the development a 27,000 square foot Memorial Grove of trees has been planted in Miller's honor. The trees, all native to Wisconsin, include hickory, walnut, beech, sugar maple, burr oak, red oak, and white oak. In addition, native trees have been planted intermittently along the walking/fitness trail. Plaques at the base of the trees identify the species.

Bill Miller Park is unlike any other park in our community in several respects. First, the need for a park in this area had been specifically noted in Park Long Range Plans in 1981, 1985, and 1987. Second, in September 1990, a citizen petition with 118 names, was presented to the City Council in support of a neighborhood park. This was the first time organized citizen support for a park helped to create a park where one was clearly needed. Third, three-fourths of the neighborhood that would benefit from the park (the area just north of the Mahler Farm) already was developed and filled with people willing to petition the Council for a neighborhood park.

The Park Commission liked the idea of a fitness trail in the Mahler Farm subdivision, but was disappointed the Bill Miller Park was limited to just three acres. That was too small to be developed in the ways that had been hoped and planned for this neighborhood park. For example, the park was too small to include a sledding hill. In a flatland like Neenah, this is a significant item to omit. The addition of three lots to the west or south of the park would have made it better able to serve the recreational needs of the neighborhood.

The idea of a fitness trail reflects the grow-

Bill Miller

ing interest in physical fitness among young and old alike. It is an attractive feature in this subdivision, but it hinders the Park Commission in developing a park that adequately serves the broader range of recreational needs.

S.F. Shattuck—A Remarkable Builder of Parks

For a period of more than sixty years, S.F. Shattuck had a quiet and influential role in the planned development of the parks of Neenah. To him belongs the credit for building much of the fine system of parks and playgrounds we enjoy in our community today.

It is difficult to find clear and unmistakable evidence of his work, for he was an exceedingly modest person. His quiet, unassuming nature tends to hide the effective leader he was. He shunned all publicity for himself, and sought no personal credit for the very beautiful parklands and swimming pool he helped create.

Shattuck was first appointed to the Neenah Park Board in June 1917. For more than thirty years, until December 1948, he served on the Park Board, most of that time as Secretary. One might expect the minutes of the Park Board to be a rich source of information about his activities as a member of the Park Board, but they are strangely silent on his own role in decisions that were made. He probably preferred it that way. As Secretary

S.F. Shattuck

he could include in the minutes only what he felt was necessary and important. He left few clues of his own actions to help any future historian determine Shattuck's personal role in decisions of the Park Board.

It is possible Shattuck may have gained an interest in parklands from his father, for F.C. Shattuck had been a member of the Park Board in the 1890s. The first firm evidence of the son's role in park development appears in 1915 on a warranty deed for the property his mother, Clara Shattuck, gave to the city as Shattuck Park. Shattuck was well aware the city would do little to develop the site as a park, even if it was given the land as a gift. He probably helped to convince his mother that if she wanted to make the site a place of beauty, she would have to develop the park herself to make her dream come true. He was always sensitive to the political realities and economic limitations of city government. It would have been very unlike him to have ignored what the city was likely to do if it were given a tract of raw land for a park.

Shattuck Park is the only one of our eighteen city parks in Neenah that was accepted by city ordinance. (No. 332, Vol. 3) The ordinance stipulates in great detail nine conditions that are to govern the use and management of the park. Perhaps Shattuck did suggest some of the stipulations for his mother to consider.

The site that later became Doty Park was the second city park to show evidence of Shattuck as a park developer. The gift of land "for park and playground purposes" was mostly wetland and cattail marsh. It was not easy for the public to get to it. A single sentence in Shattuck's HISTORY OF NEENAH suggests what he may have done (or persuaded others to do). "A group of individuals added to Mr. Clark's gift by purchase of several frontage lots on Lincoln Street . . . ." This may seem insignificant, but it reveals 1) Shattuck knew about the enhancement of the original gift of land. This was unlikely to have been common knowledge. 2) He recognized the need for land on Lincoln Street to give better public access to the park.

Washington Park, a gift to the city from Sara Bergstrom, was the next park to show Shattuck's practical approach to park development. Bergstrom specifically asked for Shattuck to represent the Park Board in negotiations for the park. No one in the city was better suited to the task.

In 1931 Sara Bergstrom wanted to give $15,000 to the city for the purchase of a suitable site for a park and playground. Shattuck realized the $15,000 might be enough to buy the land for a park, but it would not be sufficient to pay for development and beautification of the park. So he carefully drafted the terms of the gift so that development of the park was immediately assured.

Figure 46.   Shattuck and Clark's gift to Neenah swimmers.

He urged Sara Bergstrom to provide that $10,000 of the gift be used toward the purchase of the land, with the city to appropriate $5000 to complete the purchase price. That left $5000 of her gift available for design and building the park.

Shattuck knew that if there were no funds for development of the park, it would likely remain a useless, ugly patch of weeds. He knew, too, that it would be almost impossible to pry development funds from the city in that terrible worst year of the depression, 1932.

So the gift was made on terms the city could not refuse. The happy result was a public park in a part of the city where there were none. Everyone, including the donor, was delighted with the outcome.

Had it not been for his keen understanding of the practical problems of getting the city to help pay part of the costs for the creation of Washington Park, the building of the park might have been delayed for years. Shattuck had great skill in helping people accomplish difficult goals under what might have seemed impossible conditions. This park is a lasting tribute to the generosity of a great lady, and to the skill and ingenuity of a remarkable builder of parks.

Recreation Park, with its beautiful fifty meter outdoor swimming pool on the shores of Lake Winnebago, was the next park Shattuck quietly helped to build. In 1939 C.B. Clark and Shattuck anonymously offered to help the city build an Olympic size outdoor swimming pool on a site just south of the old public swimming beach on Lake Winnebago. They proposed to donate a choice lake shore site to the city. They also agreed to contribute

$52,000 toward the cost of the pool if the city would provide $25,000 toward the project. The balance of the cost, $63,000, was provided by a grant from the Public Works Administration.

Shattuck was an exceedingly generous person, generous with his own time, and talents, and wealth. However, he firmly believed any private gifts for a public park or pool should always be linked with some public commitment to the same project. This was based on the sound principle that we tend to value and respect that which we have helped (even indirectly) to create.

Repeatedly in his efforts to build parks, his belief in this principle of public commitment may be seen. It helps to account for the strong feelings of pride many of us have toward our parks. It is an attitude that tends to foster greater respect for public property.

Shattuck was a man of many talents, not the least of which was his extraordinary ability to help people from different communities and backgrounds to work together successfully to attain a common goal. He was one of the prime movers for regional planning in the Fox Valley. In 1945 he helped establish the first committee for joint urban planning in this part of Wisconsin. His widespread contacts with civic and political leaders in the Valley were invaluable in forming first the Fox Valley Planning Commission, later the Fox Valley Council of Governments, and finally the East Central Wisconsin Regional Planning Commission.

Shattuck's interest in regional planning grew from his experience with park planning and development. He undoubtedly saw that good urban planning made it easier to site parks where they were most needed by the most people. Good urban planning helps guide a community toward a more equitable distribution of parks and playgrounds, anticipates where future problems may develop, and attempts to take remedial action to avoid problems even before they occur. All these and more the planner of parks could see would make his work easier.

In 1965 the Tolverson property just east of the Neenah Public Library was up for sale. It was small, only about half an acre, but it had 120 feet of shoreline on the Fox River. It might have gone to some private developer had not Shattuck and his wife promptly bought the land and given it to the City. They recognized it was worth far more to the community as a small park, than for it to be put to any other use. Once again our community is indebted to Mr. and Mrs. Shattuck for creating and protecting a small bit of open space for all to enjoy.

Shattuck did not limit his park building efforts to his own home town. He saw the possibilities of developing the High Cliff area on the northeast shores of Lake Winnebago into a state park. He worked quietly and persistently for a good many years in cooperation with other Fox Valley leaders to help create High Cliff State Park.

The limestone cliffs overlooking Lake Winnebago had for years drawn thousands of visitors from all over eastern Wisconsin. Spectacular rock formations, huge fissures in the cliffs, unusual table-like ledges projecting above tall trees, panoramic views of the lake from the cliffs—all combined to make this a very attractive natural area.

Shattuck saw High Cliff's great potential as "a pleasuring ground for the people." He was particularly effective in helping to raise money to develop High Cliff into a state park. Often on fine summer afternoons he would organize impromptu excursions across the lake aboard his yacht, the Pilgrim. He would take people on short hikes around the cliffs so they could see for themselves why he found it to have such exciting possibilities for a state park.

In 1953 when the Wisconsin Conservation Commission wondered whether the people of the Fox Valley really needed or wanted a park, the Commission asked them to prove their interest by raising a challenge fund of $25,000 to be used for buildings and equipment when and if the park should be brought into being. Shattuck helped Chairman Gordon Bubolz of the High Cliff Forest Park Association raise more than $26,000 to meet that challenge.

Immediately upon the decision of the Wisconsin Conservation Commission to undertake the High Cliff Park project, it became obvious that a small-boat marina was a "must." There are very few safe harbors on the eastern shores of Lake Winnebago. During the summer of 1954, and again in 1957, a committee of boaters (Shattuck among them) made soundings along the shoreline and chose a spot which they considered suitable for a harbor.

An engineering firm from Sturgeon Bay was then brought in to make their own investigations and submit a price for construction of a harbor. After making their depth soundings, they brought up their probing equipment to find out what was under the floor of the lake at that point. As they probed, they were puzzled. As they worked out from shore, they had to go down through a bed of soft silt—ten, twenty, thirty feet—before finding solid bottom. The committee, too, had been mystified. They consulted Dr. Bill Reed, geologist of Lawrence University. Reed asked, "Why didn't you come to me first? You are in the bed of a prehistoric river. If you want a harbor, you'll have to go [northwest] along the bend of the lake into the clay bank and dig one."

When it came to building the marina, the Conservation Commission found themselves without money which they could put into a harbor or marina. So Shattuck and his friends went to work and raised more than $170,000 from more than 800 individuals and firms of the Fox Valley, including Oshkosh and Fond du Lac, and the present harbor eventually took shape.

It is clear that, without substantial private help, High Cliff State Park would have developed, but much more slowly than it did. Fortunately Shattuck's skill in raising funds for park development and beautification were readily available. He knew who to ask for assistance, what companies to ask for contributions. His own enthusiasm for the park encouraged givers to be generous.

Shattuck's success as a builder of parks was due in no small measure to his willingness to work without receiving personal credit or recognition for what he achieved. This is not easy to do. One must feel secure and confident in one's own self-worth to act as he did. Most of Shattuck's life was one of selfless dedication to public service. Our community would be a better place to live, and work, and play if more of us emulated S.F. Shattuck.

Appendix A

Neenah City Map Showing Parks

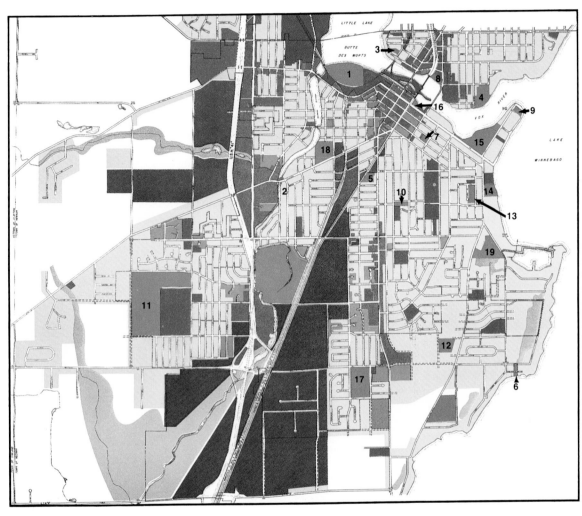

The Parks of Neenah

1 - Arrowhead Park
2 - Baldwin Park
3 - Cook Park
4 - Doty Park
5 - Douglas Park
6 - Fresh Air Camp
7 - The Green
8 - Island Park
9 - Kimberly Point Park
10 - Laudan Park

11 - Memorial Park
12 - Bill Miller Park
13 - Quarry Park
14 - Recreation Park
15 - Riverside Park
16 - Shattuck Park
17 - Southview Park
18 - Washington Park
19 - Wilderness Park

LAND USE PLAN
1986 - 2005
- L E G E N D -

☐ Low Density Residential

☐ High Density Residential

☐ Commercial

☐ Industrial

☐ Community Facilities

☐ Parks and Recreation

☐ Environmentally Sensitive Areas

☐ Undeveloped Areas

====== Proposed Streets

EAST CENTRAL WISCONSIN
REGIONAL PLANNING COMMISSION

Figure 47.   Neenah city map showing park locations.

Appendix B

Aerial Photographs

Figure 48.   Aerial view of Riverside Park (1990).

Figure 49. Aerial view of Doty Park (1990).

Figure 50. Aerial view of Kimberly Point Park (1979).

Figure 51.   Aerial view of Washington Park (1990).

Figure 52. Aerial view of Island and Shattuck Parks. (1990)

Figure 53.   Aerial view of Rec and Quarry Parks (1990).

Figure 54. Aerial view of Memorial Park (1990).

Figure 55.   Aerial view of Southview Park (1990).

Figure 56. Aerial view of Wilderness Park (1990).

Figure 57. Aerial view of Arrowhead Park (1990).